# Unfolding

*Thirty-One Days of Finding Encouragement in the Words of Our Personal God*

Sarah Deal

ISBN 979-8-89112-295-6 (Paperback)
ISBN 979-8-89112-297-0 (Hardcover)
ISBN 979-8-89112-296-3 (Digital)

Copyright © 2024 Sarah Deal
All rights reserved
First Edition

Scripture quotations from
The Holy Bible, English Standard Version® ( ESV®)
Copyright © 2001 by Crossway,
a publishing ministry of Good News Publishers.
All rights reserved.

All rights reserved. No part of this publication may be reproduced, distributed, or transmitted in any form or by any means, including photocopying, recording, or other electronic or mechanical methods without the prior written permission of the publisher. For permission requests, solicit the publisher via the address below.

Covenant Books
11661 Hwy 707
Murrells Inlet, SC 29576
www.covenantbooks.com

I love words. There's a power to the written word that can inform, educate, heal, encourage, relate, and strengthen. But the power doesn't come from the words themselves, not from their letters and symbols or their languages and the cultures that lie beautiful and complex in layers behind them.

No, the power in written words comes from the Creator of life itself, and the one who breathed his life into man, making male and female in his image with creativity and a desire to communicate and make sense of the world he created.

And that same God chose, at just the perfect time in history, to preserve his Word through men, who wrote down his words and passed them down to us so that we, too, could know his thoughts and his heart. God loves words too! And as we come to his Word, as we unfold the pages of his heart and his character, we find wisdom and light for our own story. It's how we make sense of our own world and our own journeys. It's in his words that we find the unfolding of our own purpose within his grand design.

I invite you to join me on my journey into the unfolding as I've sought to come to God's Word, asking him to give me wisdom and insight into my own story. I pray you are blessed and encouraged, as I have been, knowing that God is intimately involved with every step of your unfolding story.

# Day 1

*We do not know what to do, but our eyes are on you.*
—2 Chronicles 20:12

As a chronic overthinker, I am asking the Lord to remind me to start my days (and intersperse them!) with this cry.

Yes, Lord.

With all my reasoning, all my pondering and anxious figuring, I still don't know what to do. I set my eyes on him, the One who knows the way and the answer to all my wondering.

Oh, how I need this reminder *daily*!

# Day 2

*And Hezekiah spoke encouragingly to all the Levites who showed good skill in the service of the Lord.*
—2 Chronicles 30:22

Our oldest son just started ninth grade yesterday. When he was in second grade, I was his teacher for a year of homeschooling during a home assignment year. A history class project required him to interview me about how we picked his name and why. How embarrassing.

For the life of me, I couldn't think of anything deep to tell the kid. The baby name website was no help either, giving me some lame definition including a dog in its ridiculous description.

I bring this up because mothers like me were rare, if not nonexistent, in Biblical times. Names were extremely important and held deep clues and messages for those who were looking for insight and wisdom from God.

Lately, I've found a new favorite character in the Old Testament, and his name means "Yahweh [the Lord] strengthens." Hezekiah came on the scene at a time of conflict and political upheaval in both Israel and Judah, and God raised him up to be king over the people of Judah. Second Chronicles 29–32 give details of Hezekiah's reign, how he walked faithfully before the Lord and led both Israel and Judah into worship and obedience to Yahweh once again. Although his life was not free from struggle or sin, one thing is certain: Hezekiah lives up to his name. He allows the Lord to strengthen the people through him, encouraging them in their service as he leads.

I am struck by this simple yet profound act of Hezekiah's leadership.

He speaks encouragingly to the Levites who were serving, who were *only* doing what they were meant to do. What was expected of them. Yet he stops. He takes time to speak words of encouragement to them.

Later in in the same verse, we read that this leads to them giving thanks to the Lord!

And repeatedly in these chapters, I noticed a pattern of Hezekiah's leadership—he encourages, and the people are filled with joy, with praise, with thanksgiving.

What is the challenge for my own life? Am I quick to speak encouragingly to those around me who are faithfully serving the Lord? If not, what is stopping me? Am I afraid of making others too proud? Am I afraid of feeling smaller somehow in comparison?

O Lord, make me a reflection of you, willing to encourage and strengthen my sisters and brothers as they serve you faithfully around me!

# Day 3

*For this light momentary affliction is preparing for us an eternal weight of glory beyond all comparison.*
—2 Corinthians 4:17

He never wastes a thing.

    I am often tempted to believe the lie that today's wrestling and struggle will not amount to much: when things don't make sense, when I can't draw a straight line between my struggle and his glory, and when I feel like no one else understands the tension in my heart. Can I trust that this very struggle and tension that I live with today is a part of a weight that will matter in eternity? A recent "light and momentary affliction" is an interpersonal conflict that has dragged on for the better part of a year. I've felt alone, misunderstood, hurt, mistreated, and angry. God has worked relentlessly on my heart as I've come face-to-face with many of my fears, from owning up to my wrong attitudes in front of people who intimidate me, to sitting quietly while I hear the consequences of my passive anger in others' lives being laid open and bare in my presence.

    God has shown me more of himself, of his deep love, of his unending mercy, of his grace, of how much that I lack, of how I fall short so often in giving that grace and love to others, of how insincere I truly am at my core, in my deepest parts, of how needy I am of his amazingly steady grace.

He is showing me how incredibly impossible it is to love in my own strength. I just can't do it. Only in him can I truly love, forgive, be humble, be sincere, be kind, be merciful.

And what of this affliction? Wasted? The deceiver lies in wait to snatch the truth from my heart, to tempt me with thoughts that God will turn his back on the mess of my moments and that the knots of entanglement surrounding my sin are too much for him to redeem. But, oh, the truth unfolds in my heart, and I praise him for his grace! This affliction—light in comparison to the weight of glory—is not enough to keep him from me!

And this affliction—momentary compared to eternity—is not enough to separate me from his love! You see, he's preparing for us an eternal weight of glory not because we are worthy but because he is worthy. And every affliction we face here he uses to humble and redeem.

To transform us into his image and to draw us closer to himself because that's what a good Father, a good God does.

He never wastes a thing.

# Day 4

*Do not take to heart all the things that people say, lest you hear your servant cursing you. Your heart knows that many times you yourself have cursed others. All this I have tested by wisdom. I said, "I will be wise," but it was far from me.*

—Ecclesiastes 7:21–23

In my devotions, I've been working my way through the Old Testament and just recently wrapped up the story of David in 2 Samuel. As I jumped into 1 Kings this morning and read of Solomon's rise to the throne and his request for wisdom, I was challenged to read through some of his writings in the book of Ecclesiastes.

Although I don't have a servant, and I wouldn't necessarily say I go around fearing people are cursing me, I *do* have an issue with reading into people's opinions of me. I worry too much about what others think or say and take it to heart as if their views define me. I love Solomon's divinely inspired wisdom here. Don't take it to heart.

Remember the source. We are all just fallen humans, who give in to temptation and say things we shouldn't, think things we shouldn't. Remember,

Sarah, you are not always wise in your dealings with others.

Remember to forgive when someone seems to treat you unfairly. Set your soul's worth and value on firm footing—with Christ. That's the only place where you're sure to find that unshakable, always welcoming, never-changing grace, 100 percent of the time!

This is wisdom at its finest.

# Day 5

*Therefore take up the whole armor of God,
that you may be able to withstand in the evil
day, and having done all, to stand firm.*
—*Ephesians 6:13*

My hubby is faithful in a lot of things. He flosses every night. He always empties the coffee filter. He always wipes the toilet seat. And he always, *always*, wears his motorcycle gear when he goes on a ride.

And this weekend, it saved him a *lot* of hurt. Those few extra moments to put on the heavy jacket, strap up thick elbow and knee pads, pull on the stretchy, hard-knuckled gloves, and tighten up that bulky helmet were well worth the effort. The gear did its job and protected him when he hit a deer and slid on a remote gravel road, leaving him, miraculously, with only a few minor injuries.

As I sat with him in the ER on Saturday, amazed at how few scratches he had after such an ordeal, my mind came to rest on Paul's exhortation in Ephesians 6.

Put on the whole armor of God.

A command that calls for faithfulness, just as Shad's gear would have done him no good sitting at home in the closet, so the armor of God does me no good if I don't take the time to put it on.

My reflection begged the question: Do I make the effort to put it on?

As I fasten my belt, I pray, "Lord, I choose to trust what you say is truth, no matter what I am feeling at the moment."

As I put on my shirt, I pray, "Lord, I cling to you as my righteousness, the One who has said there is no condemnation because of your finished work on the cross for me!"

As I put on my shoes, I pray, "Lord, help me to walk today ready to share your gospel of peace with others and sure of it myself!"

As I put on my jewelry (work with me here!), I pray, "Lord, in faith, I believe that I am who you say I am, forgiven and loved because of your sacrifice."

As I do my hair, I pray, "Lord, I praise you for your salvation, which is eternal and sure!"

As I read his Word, I pray, "Lord, help me to take your Word to heart—to not just hear it but to live it, to believe it, and allow you to transform me into your image! Where there is sin in my heart, expose it."

And as I put on, as I pray and am alert and ready for battle, I can be assured of one thing: battle will come.

Injuries are highly likely.

But the armor was designed to protect, and to allow the warrior to continue to engage in battle until his (or her!) time is done.

# Day 6

*But many of the priests and Levites and heads of fathers' houses, old men who had seen the first house, wept with a loud voice when they saw the foundation of this house being laid, though many shouted aloud for joy.*

—*Ezra 3:12*

Forgive me if some of my raw emotion has spilled over onto you recently. This is an area that is hard and real and not one that's easy to hide from those who let me into their world, nor from those whom I allow into mine. I'm learning that grief doesn't have a timeline, that it's messy and subtle and sometimes stays hidden until you least expect it.

I was recently struck by this little verse, tucked away in a beautiful story of captives being reunited in the book of Ezra. Amid the rebuilding of the foundation of the Temple where God would dwell, there was much rejoicing. The returning, the reuniting, the answered prayers—it all culminated in a cry that God was good, that his steadfast love endures forever (v. 11).

Yet still, God, in his sovereignty, saw fit to preserve in his Word this detail of the grief of the old men. The ones who had lived to see the glory of what once was, and thus had something to grieve that day.

Something to unpack that the young ones had not tasted.

Yes, grief often feels that way.

Awkward.

Out of place in the middle of rejoicing.

Misunderstood.

Yet I chew on this, and I am deeply moved by my gentle Savior, who sits with me while I process my grief layer upon layer as it bubbles up in my heart.

Even when it's inconvenient.

Even when no one gets it.

Yes, even when it's, well, awkward.

Even when it's hard to distinguish between the shout of joy and the cry of grieving, rest assured that one truth stands above it all.

Our God is good.

His steadfast love endures forever, in every season of our lives. In joy, in suffering, in grief, and in relief, he is ever-present and ever-caring.

# Day 7

*But the* Lord *was with Joseph and showed him steadfast love and gave him favor in the sight of the keeper of the prison.*

*—Genesis 39:21*

Sometimes it is hard to make sense of what God is doing. I'd venture to say that if we were to pull up a chair and invite some Old Testament characters over for coffee, they'd agree that it's often hard to make sense of God's plan.

I've recently been reviewing the story of Joseph, in all its twists and turns. He's certainly one of those who could attest to the fact that the road on the way to God's plans is full of surprises!

One detail in Joseph's story that stuck out to me as I was reading this week was this little phrase that kept popping up: "The Lord was with Joseph."

When he was sold into slavery, ripped away from all he'd ever known, with no promise of ever returning: "The Lord was with Joseph" (39:2).

When he was thrown in prison, falsely accused after being faithful to his master and doing what was right: "The Lord was with Joseph."

When I step back and take a good look at the context of this phrase in Joseph's story, it challenges me.

On days when things aren't going well, I tend to think God isn't near, that he's somewhere else, probably with those who are enjoying success or more fruit in ministry. But I hear in Joseph's story the whisper of God's voice: "Sarah, I am with you."

On the days I can't see his plan, on the days I struggle with feeling alone or misunderstood, on the days when he feels far away, what was true in Joseph's story is true in mine, the Lord is with me.

So tonight, I choose to lean into that truth.

No matter how loud the voices outside (or inside) try to convince me otherwise. He is with me. Christ lives within me! He has a plan. From every twist and turn, he will get the glory.

(See also 2 Timothy 1:12.)

# Day 8

*And I will have mercy on No Mercy, and I will say to Not My People, "You are my people;" and he shall say, "You are my God."*

—Hosea 2:23

This week, I had my first migraine in months. I woke up in the wee hours of the morning on Sunday with the room spinning and a nauseating headache barging its way into my peaceful night's sleep.

I tried to ignore it, managed to push through the day, and ended up making things worse, which left me feeling pretty much useless on Sunday evening and well into Monday.

My three men cared for me and fended for themselves while I laid low for the good part of Sunday night and Monday.

Shad said it's what I needed.

But I hate being unproductive. Not that I don't enjoy a day of relaxation every now and then, but there's just something about lying on the couch and watching your family function without you that's, well, humbling, hard, guilt-inducing.

It felt lazy, self-serving, useless.

In the intense cloudiness of the migraine haze, even praying and reading scripture seemed out of reach and impossible.

As the moments ticked away and the migraine fog began to clear, I was struck with this thought: I so desperately feel this tension inside myself each moment to prove something, to prove my worth in what I do and what I can accomplish. Even as I lay sick, my mind was preoccupied with how to prove I was worth something. Today, I was reminded in scripture of the story of Hosea. These words are a beautiful reminder to my heart that God calls us and defines us on *his* terms, not our own.

Mercy for the one called no mercy.

His people for those who were not his people.

As he drew out his children in the days of Israel, calling them to repentance and trust in his name, and as he called Hosea's unfaithful wife to return to him, so he calls us and draws us gently to himself.

He has already decided who we are. He has already defined me, and this will not change. I can trust him with my moments, resting secure in the fact that I don't need to prove myself to him. The difference this makes in my heart is vast—I serve him from a heart of love and not compulsion and his light shines through me—cracks and all, to the world as I trust and rest in his righteousness and his work apart from my own.

When I have nothing to offer, he loves me and names me his own. Yes, even in the middle of my migraine!

# Day 9

*Why do you say "My way is hidden from the LORD,*
*and my right is disregarded by my God?"*
*Have you not known? Have you not heard?*
*The Lord is the everlasting God, the Creator of the ends*
*of the earth...his understanding is unsearchable.*

—Isaiah 40:27–28

A friend brought me a beautiful marigold plant a few weeks ago, a sweet gesture of kindness that was greatly appreciated. She didn't realize that my house is where plants come to die. You see, I don't do well with plants or pets—I've always done better to just stick with keeping my kids fed with enough canned veggies to outweigh their newfound love of Little Debbie's.

The only reason I knew this beautiful flower was a marigold was because my mom used to have a row of them out behind our back porch. When they would shrivel and die in the Florida sun, their little pathetic-looking appendages would fall to the ground, releasing dozens of tiny seeds that would produce a whole new harvest of beautiful marigolds.

As a girl, it fascinated me.

So you can imagine my relief when, as per usual, my beautiful plant began to droop and wilt in the Missouri sun. I recognized right away the life-giving seeds, disguised in a shade of pathetic brown.

I waited, and I watched.

I watered my plant.

I wondered if it would spring back to life.

Sure enough, I went out one morning to find my pot bursting with shoots of green, followed some time after with promising buds. Finally, brilliant bursts of orange crowded and filled my pot, until I had no choice but to split it in two and give some back to my friend who was first to share it with me.

The lesson? Are we not like the marigold? I know I often feel my plight is hidden before the Lord. Does he see when I'm shriveled and feeling low? Is there promise, are there good days yet to come?

Oh, the hope in his Word! Have you not heard? He is the everlasting God! Nothing escapes his understanding. He gets it, whatever we're walking through, and he's right in the thick of it with us. Even when it looks like we've withered up, reached the end of an era, when grief is thick and heavy, there is hope in our everlasting God who knows no end.

There's hope, friends. I'm *so* very grateful for this God, the God, *my* God, who understands and walks with us through the seasons of our lives.

There's always hope and always time to bloom.

# Day 10

*He delivers the afflicted by their affliction
and opens their ear by adversity.*

—*Job 36:15*

Wouldn't it be nice if we always got what we wanted?

I've been wrestling with this a lot lately, wishing God would somehow get the memo and get on board with my plans of how I'd like my day, my week, even my life, to go.

Yet, true to his gracious character, he challenges me through his Word. I recently finished the story of Job in my morning reading, and man, has it hit me hard! I've been reflecting on this little verse in particular for the past week, and it has brought some much-needed perspective.

My affliction, in whatever form, is designed to draw me closer to him. To make me more aware of my need for him, to help me to hear his voice above all other voices. When I focus solely on the struggle, big or small, I miss the opportunity to hear him, to see him for who he is—the One who can meet the needs that are currently not being met through whatever disappointment I am facing. This is what I want, and this is what I need! I want to hear you, Lord, in my good days and on the days I struggle. What a good God you are, that even in the affliction, you are drawing me close and delivering me.

# Day 11

*But Jesus on his part did not entrust himself
to them, because he knew all people.*

—*John 2:24*

My eleven-year-old asked me nonchalantly the other day who my best friend was. After eliminating my predictable answers of Shad and Jesus, Brice patiently waited as I reflected for a good long while. It was hard to answer.

Don't get me wrong. I have friends. There are many people in my life I enjoy—share life with and laugh, pray, cry with. Our life's work requires that we pour in and out.

But a best friend?

A best friend requires that I am known—deeply known and accepted. There's a sense of identity involved in finding and holding on to a best friend.

Today, I spent some time in the familiar first two chapters of the gospel of John and was struck by this thought of Jesus being known.

To be more accurate, Jesus not being known.

He made the world, but it did not know him (1:10). He came to his own, but they did not receive him (1:11).

It is with this backdrop that we come to the end of chapter two, where we read these words of Jesus, that he did not entrust himself to those in Jerusalem who believed in his name simply because of what he could do for them.

His identity did not depend on the masses, on those who would define him based on how his presence improved their lives at the moment.

What of me? How quickly do I entrust my identity in the hands of others? And does my identity, my felt need to be known, even matter? He definitely understands the struggle of being misunderstood, unaccepted, unknown. He's a compassionate High Priest who meets us in our weakness (Hebrews 4:15).

And in the wrestling, as I seek to surrender my own selfishness and pride to his will and his sovereignty in my life, I am reminded of the words of the prophet in Jeremiah 9:24: "Let him who boasts boast in this, that he understands and knows me, that I am the LORD who practices steadfast love, justice, and righteousness in the earth. For in these things I delight, declares the LORD."

As the disciples, I seek to follow his call to "Come and see"—to learn more of him every day and be willing to let who I am be swallowed up by who he is. May I not be like those Jerusalem masses who clung to Jesus simply because of the tangible benefits he gave them at the moment and when he made them well and full and famous. May I entrust my identity to him even when it means going unnoticed and unknown and demands swallowing my pride.

Sorry, Brice. I'm sticking with my original answer. Jesus is my best friend.

# Day 12

*He must increase but I must decrease.*

*—John 3:30*

Recently, I had the privilege of speaking to a group of ladies who are near and dear to my heart. We spent a beautiful, sunny, breezy Saturday together in God's Word, enjoying good fellowship, worship, and food. Someone managed to snap this picture during one of my sessions, and it spoke a sweet, strong, yet subtle whisper to my heart.

Be content to live in the background, to minister in the shadow, to allow God's Word and his Truth to shine so bright that *he* is what is seen and what is in focus when others look in my direction.

As I serve, may I be keenly aware that I am his instrument, tuned for his use.

May my passion be poured into those relationships, those tasks that he has called me to, and may others see in me his love and his grace more than they see, well, me.

# Day 13

*And the Lord said, "Do you do well to be angry?"*
—*Jonah 4.4*

Today, I yelled at God. I was alone in the car on the way to do my grocery run.

I cried, too. Hard. I drove an extra twenty minutes to make an extra stop to give my puffy, red face time to return to its normal hue. I'm not proud of it. I was truly ticked—ticked that God's sovereignty didn't buy me a ticket to all my expectations, frustrated that he seemed to turn his back on me when I really needed him to come through. Hurt that he added one more thing to what felt like an already full punch card of stresses in this particular season.

A few days ago, my reading brought me to the familiar story of Jonah, who, like myself, was acquainted with the emotion of anger. After my errand outburst, I was drawn to review Jonah's own outburst in Jonah 4. The context encouraged me as I sought to see the age-old story with fresh eyes.

Jonah is angry, and the Lord asks him (loosely translated): "Jonah, do you have a reason to be angry?"

The way I always imagined it was that the Lord proceeds to put Jonah in his place by sending a plant and a worm, and Jonah never really learns his lesson.

But as I read it again, something different struck me. The Lord could have walked away at the beginning of Jonah's struggle, after verse 4, without any further teaching or clarification. Jonah wasn't owed anything by God, and he certainly could have just left Jonah there to wallow alone or get his attitude right before engaging him further.

I know this is how I often feel God views me, as if he's waiting for me to get my act together, to first clean up my motives and toe the line before I can even approach him.

But here, nestled in this Old Testament, pre-Christ book, we find the graciousness of God and glimpses of his patience as he seeks his own.

Notice how God goes after Jonah. He appoints a plant to save him from discomfort. Then he appoints a worm to attack the plant. Then he appoints a scorching east wind and sun to beat down on Jonah's head, so he was faint. As far as I can tell, all these things God appointed, not for the world, not for those Jonah was appointed to prophesy to, but for an angry, disgruntled man. One whom he loved and who was worth teaching and pursuing.

The takeaway for me is this: when I am angry, I need not run from him. When his truth exposes my sinful heart, I need not fear condemnation, for I am loved and pursued and known by my Creator. May my days end in surrender to the One whose shoulders are wide enough to handle all my pain and anger yet loving enough to never let me be satisfied with anything less than him.

# Day 14

*"The Lord is my portion," says my soul,*
*"therefore I will hope in him."*

—Lamentations 3:24

Not gonna lie. The past week or so has been brutal—COVID-19, aches, pains, coughs, headaches, backaches, fevers.

Prayers and tears. Lots and lots of tears.

Exhaustion, fatigue, and discouragement.

Then there were the texts. The daily check-ins from friends. The emails and Facebook messages from those who knew our situation and just wanted us to know they cared.

Meals and groceries followed, as well as regular mail drops and even a bouquet of flowers to cheer our quarantined souls. And prayers, so many prayers, have been lifted on our behalf by friends and family who love us more than we deserve.

Through this time, God has reminded us again of the lessons of lament.

What is my portion? What do I have to look forward to in this life when my plans come crashing down and when a virus invades my life and my comfort and my well-being?

Yes, the Lord, he is my portion! Though I praise him for the ways he uses good things and people in my life to bring comfort, ultimately, *he* is the One who is my portion and my inheritance in this life, the only One at the end of the day and at the end of life who can sustain and satisfy my soul!

And where is my hope? My hope does not lie in getting God to answer a prayer my way. I will hope in him because he is completely and utterly trustworthy. I can trust him to be good, even when I feel like he's left me out to dry.

Pain and lament have a way of helping us wrestle through these issues honestly with the Lord, and I am thankful. Thankful that he has been so patient with me as I've wrestled through this virus and learned anew the importance of identifying my true hope and portion.

# Day 15

*Restore us to yourself, O Lord that we may
be restored! Renew our days as of old.*
—Lamentations 5:21

Lately, I've been longing for simpler times: when my boys were little and we were living a life I'd pictured across the ocean; a time previrus, when the world didn't seem so complicated and divided by politics and agendas; when gas prices weren't rising so rapidly, along with inflation like I haven't seen in my lifetime.

Now there's so many things unsure, so many things complicated. I feel like Jeremiah, the author of Lamentations, could relate to my longings and my grief.

He, too, had lost much and spent five whole chapters spilling out his grief to God (and eventually the literate world after him). I find deep comfort in this next to the last verse of his book of lament.

A plea for restoration and renewal, but not one I would naturally expect from a man wrestling through grief. He prays first, not for restoration of wealth or status, of the kingdom or control. His prayer is simply this: Restore us to yourself, O Lord.

Yes, herein lies the challenge. This is where restoration needs to happen first. In turning my heart, my eyes back to him, to his grace and his goodness and his sovereign control of every situation I encounter.

A surrender of my right to understand his plan.

A surrender of my right to have life go as I planned.

A surrender of my right to always be understood.

An invitation to lean in and draw close to the One who made me and calls me and understands my heart. This restoration is taking hold of what Christ has already finished on my behalf on the cross—that I may be restored (returned, brought back to God).

Come what may, in the dark and in the day, he is the anchor and the hope that I can rest in.

The note he ends on gives the final punch to this section: Renew our days as of old. It's reminiscent of Psalm 139:5: "You hem me in, behind and before..." The same Hebrew word is used in both of these verses for "old" and "before," reinforcing this picture that God has been there in the past and goes with us in the future. I love this picture that God is not satisfied to just reinvent exact replicas of the awesome things he has done in the past to show his faithfulness but has promised to make all things new, according to the way he revealed himself in the past.

And so today, as I look back on seemingly simpler times, I choose to recount his faithfulness in those moments and those days. And I choose to look for his grace and his goodness today, too, because I know it's right here, waiting for me. It always will be because he is a God of renewal and a God of restoration.

# Day 16

*And they came to Jesus and saw the demon-possessed man, the one who had had the legion, sitting there, clothed and in his right mind, and they were afraid.*
*—Mark 5:15*

Fear. It's an emotion I know well.
   Fear of the future.
   Fear of war.
   Fear of financial ruin.
   Fear of people's opinions.
   Fear of being misunderstood.
   And yes, I'll even admit to having my fair share of fear of missing out.
   Fear is a great leveler, a foe that seems to haunt all that walk this earth.
   Were we created to fear? Made to quiver and squirm under circumstances outside our control?
   I am challenged by this story in scripture, where we read of a fear brought on by an unexpected catalyst—an unlikely miracle, a freeing act of mercy, an outworking of God's abundant grace to a man in desperate need of just that.
   When the people saw the demon-possessed man, walking around, free and in his right mind, they were afraid, not relieved or thankful or reflective.

It's easy, sitting here in the twenty-first century, to judge these ones who feared in the face of the transforming touch of Jesus and the radical outpouring and change it brought in the lives of those around him.

But what of me?

Do I welcome the transformational change the Holy Spirit offers in my daily life (Romans 12:2)? Am I leery of the effect his transforming power will have on my comfort, my reputation, or my relationships?

O God, may my heart be so aligned with yours that your will becomes my desire, regardless of how radically it shakes up my normal! May I resist the urge to fear losing perceived control, fearing only you and recognizing your sovereignty in every corner of my life and my moments.

And in the end, knowing who is standing with me, what do I really have to fear?

# Day 17

*If you then, who are evil, know how to give good gifts to your children, how much more will your Father who is in heaven give good things to those who ask him!*

—*Matthew 7:11*

Yesterday evening, I spent five hours doing homework with my fourteen-year-old son. He sheepishly asked me to help him after realizing he had let the weekend pass by without completing the majority of his first pre-AP English project that was due on Tuesday morning.

We settled on the couch and laid out his materials, working together on an outline for a four to six-minute speech comparing two literary works. The hours passed quickly as we delved into the world of writing, mother and son. I gave him suggestions on word choice and connectors, and he asked for advice when he got stuck.

I genuinely enjoyed this opportunity to connect, bonding over the written word (something I *love*!). Don't get me wrong, it was a *long* evening. But truly, it was a joy to help my son with something that was a challenge for him even though it took time and energy to do so. I was thankful that he wanted my help and that he welcomed my input. By night's end, having added several words to his vocabulary, my son had transformed into quite the budding author.

"I learned this from you, Mom!" he said.

Reflecting on his words, it took all my willpower not to cry happy, proud tears. It was a poignant moment.

Here's what God challenged me with today as I reflected, *Do I sheepishly come to him for help when I'm struggling with all life requires of me? When I'm feeling overwhelmed, not enough, worn out, behind schedule, or inadequate for the task?*

If I, just a human with a limited amount of patience and time, can meet my son in the moment and give him what he needs to meet the demands of the task in front of him, how much more will my Father in heaven meet me there in my place of need?

What's more, just as my son accepted my help and, in the process, began to learn from me, so I, as I lean into dependence on my Father, will learn of him and begin to reflect his character in my life.

What a good Father! He gives such good things to us! May I never shy away from asking him to help, for he waits and takes joy in sitting beside and meeting me in my place of need, teaching me to be more like himself along the way.

# Day 18

*Take my yoke upon you, and learn from
me, for I am gentle and lowly in heart,
and you will find rest for your souls.*

*—Matthew 11:29*

There are some days when I wake up feeling particularly alone. I don't know if you've ever felt it too.

I know the truth.

I know that God is for me.

I know that he loves me.

I know that he's given me everything I need.

But some days, like today, I need that gentle reminder from my Father that he is yoked to me. More accurately, I am yoked to him. Yes, that's much better. He is my teammate, the one in my corner, always standing beside me and understanding exactly and perfectly all that goes through this complicated head of mine.

Ever-understanding.

Ever-loving.

Ever-pursuing, even when, and I dare say especially when, I least deserve it.

Ever-gracious and forgiving when I choose sin that so easily besets.

Ever-present in every up and down and in-between along the way.

Ever-teaching and drawing me to himself.

Ever-gentle in his ways.

So to anyone else who may be feeling alone in your corner today, remember that if you've come to him in faith, you are yoked to him forever! Rest assured, he's always in your corner.

Always.

People come and people go. Their opinions shift, and they'll never understand the way he does. I'm learning to let them off the hook. He made us, and he knows us like no other. He voluntarily walks each step with us not because we're worthy, but because he chooses it, and because of that, he defines us as worthy teammates of his. You don't need to live up because you're already in.

I don't know about you, but today, I needed to remember that I'm yoked, and I'm so grateful for the rest that brings to my soul.

# Day 19

*Iron sharpens iron, and one man sharpens another.*
*—Proverbs 27:17*

My husband is a knife sharpener. When he spots someone with a pocketknife, you can rest assured he will ask them about it. Midconversation, he will offer to take it home and sharpen it. Over the next few days, he will work it meticulously through two crude-looking bars of course metal, resulting in a super sharp blade.

The sound is horrendous, like nails on a chalkboard.

But like a good wife, I do my best to ignore it. I'm thankful for the blessing he is to others, but at a knife-sharpening hour, you can typically find me running for cover out of earshot of the grating hullabaloo.

Then one day, it hit me. Iron sharpening iron. I'd quoted the verse many times. It represents the way that community—specifically a community of people who know Christ, who serve and love and work together—should encourage and sharpen each other in the Lord.

But what I hadn't realized before was that typically, when iron sharpens iron, the process is less than comfortable. You see, when iron sharpens iron, it sometimes means saying hard things. Gulp. I'm more of a hugger.

And as Shad and I have spent the last fifteen years serving alongside cross-cultural workers, let me tell you, the need for encouragers is very real! During our years on the field and since we've been back in the US, we've remained convinced that there are hurting people everywhere—people who feel alone, isolated, and discouraged, people who need a meal or a note or a hug.

But as I watch Shad faithfully sharpening his knives, I'm reminded and challenged that God has called us all to be sharpeners, to be iron that sharpens iron.

Sometimes that means gently pointing out sin I see in a friend's life.

Sometimes it means having a hard conversation to preserve a relationship that has been filled with tension.

Sometimes it means risking what is comfortable for the sake of what is best.

Iron sharpening iron, willing to allow those rough edges to be shaved away in my own life to reveal a more useful instrument. More equipped to do the works the Creator has prepared in advance for me to do.

I pray I'll always be an encourager for the Lord, but these days, I'm asking him to help me step up and be willing to be iron, too.

(Adapted from a devotional originally written to be published by Thrive Connection.)

# Day 20

*But you, O L<small>ORD</small>, are a shield about me, my glory, and the lifter of my head.*

*—Psalm 3:3*

Life is messy. If I'm honest, I'll tell you that I am easily overwhelmed by the here and now, by responsibilities, relationships, expectations, and daily life that sits right in front of me.

It's easy to forget to look up.

Our oldest son was born with a curious disposition, eyes always wandering from one new thing to the next literally from the day he was born. I often found myself cradling his little face in my hands, gently forcing him to focus on me, his mother, the one who knew what was best, the one who could help him learn where to get that next bottle or how to walk or communicate his growing list of needs. I am deeply moved by my Father's care for me, as the lifter of my head. I get it. If I, as a mother, lift my son's head in an effort to direct him to a richer life, how much more does my Father long to do the same for me?

So today, I choose to submit to his gentle cupping of my face in his hands. I look to him, and I choose to focus on his face, allowing everything else to fade into the background.

# Day 21

*But you do see, for you note mischief and
vexation, that you may take it into your hands;
to you the helpless commits himself.*

—Psalm 10:14

Have you ever felt like God didn't see you? Didn't hear your prayers or your cry for help? Maybe you felt like he's forgotten you?

You're not alone.

Recently, we've been surrounded by reminders of our past life and ministry in Asia Pacific.

Six new missionaries arriving to "our" city, beginning their study of the Indonesian language and culture—another round of coworkers to begin without us there. An opportunity to give a lecture and teach a small group in the methods of language and culture acquisition—another reminder of a fulfilling ministry left behind across the ocean.

Connecting with an Indonesian church in Michigan via the web and watching their services—a reminder of the sweet friendship and fellowship left behind.

I can relate to the poignant cry of the Psalmist in chapter ten, verse one, as he cries: "Why, O Lord, do you stand far away?"

I still, over five years after Shad's brain surgery and coming off the field, wonder why. And I ask the questions: Has he forgotten? Does he hear? Does he see?

But my God doesn't leave me there. He fights for his own, strengthening my heart by reminding me of truth and of who he is.

My heart dares to believe: "But you *do* see!" He inclines his ear to hear us on our dark and foggy days when we doubt and grieve and struggle to understand his ways. He takes notice of our suffering. He is well aware of the relentless attacks of our enemy in tempting us to be discouraged, discontent, and frustrated.

Yes, he *does* see! And I can trust that he has been up to something good all along, and he never stopped caring or purposely planning the intricate details of my life. And so today, in these hours and in these moments, I choose to trust him, resting in the fact that he takes my future into his ever-capable, ever-loving hands. I commit myself to him, Helper of the helpless and Good King forever.

# Day 22

*The young lions suffer want and hunger; but those who seek the L*ORD *lack no good thing.*

*—Psalm 34:10*

I've been thinking a lot lately about God's goodness. But maybe not in the way you're thinking or expecting. Not in the neat and tidy, Sunday morning, typical Facebook post type of way.

When I sit in the stillness and really let myself wrestle with the whys and the hurts in certain chapters of my life, I'm uncomfortable with the reality of how God's goodness plays out.

That's why I've been reflecting on the heart cries of others recently, struggling too to see God's goodness in their lives. Their cries go something like this:

"God, have you forgotten me?"

"God, why have you rejected me?"

Some may argue: "Misery loves company."

Others may counter: "Throw some Truth at those hurts. Just take God at his word and all struggles will immediately evaporate."

But I must stand and disagree on behalf of the hurting and questioning hearts.

Those heart cries of pain and confusion and frustration at God's plan didn't come from places of rebellion or walking away from truth. They come directly from the pages of scripture, from a Psalmist who, in the very same verses clung to God as his Rock and his Refuge (see Psalm 42:9, 43:2).

Amid our wrestling, what can we be sure of? When I seek him, I lack no good thing. He withholds no good thing from me. Many things he may hold back, many things he asks me to wait on. But I am learning that in his goodness, he gives me what is good (by *his* definition and according to *his* infinite wisdom!) for now.

And in the struggle, he is there. He knows I will suffer, just as I know my children will sometimes suffer when I give them what they need rather than what they want. Slowly, slowly, I am learning that he is after my heart most of all—that he is jealous for me and wants me to seek after him more than anything else. This is worth the long journey for him, heartache and all. I choose today to trust him with those questions and hurts and believe that he is good, even when I don't see it.

# Day 23

*But I will sing of your strength; I will sing*
*aloud of your steadfast love in the morning.*
*For you have been to me a fortress and a*
*refuge in the day of my distress.*

—*Psalm 59:16*

Heads up.

This lady has a lot of practice putting on a happy face. It's what she does, and it comes as natural as breathing. But can I let you in on a little secret? She's struggling.

Within literally twelve hours of hubby getting staples and stitches out from his collision with a deer on a motorcycle ride last weekend, she ended up back in the ER with her fourteen-year-old waiting on an X-ray and stitches for a busted elbow after a nasty fall.

Friends, this is the metaphorical tip of the iceberg of the emotional tension in my heart these days.

I am reminded often in this season of how weak I am. Despite the smile you see, I am often trembling inside. I am not strong in myself. I feel unable to handle even the seemingly small interruptions and ordeals that come waltzing into the tidy little world I'm trying frantically to keep in order. At times I even lie awake at night, scheming about how to maneuver things in such a way so that I can feel normal again—with stresses and pressures lightened and only dishes and laundry and some semblance of normal life to maintain.

But my Father reminds me that these tight places he allows and orchestrates are designed to remind me that dependence on him is what's he's after.

Strength, true strength, comes from *him* and not from me. Strength doesn't come from normalcy.

Not from monotony.

Not from predictability.

Not in an uninterrupted schedule.

Not from a year (or even a month!) without an ER visit.

Not in a confidence that Sarah and her smile are enough to conquer the world.

My prayer is that he may be glorified as I continue to recognize my utter need for him as my Refuge in every corner of my life and choose to rejoice in HIS strength.

# Day 24

*Enter his gates with thanksgiving,*
*and his courts with praise!*

—*Psalm 100.4*

In 2021, our family had the opportunity to spend some time at a retreat designed to help us unpack and process some of our journey in overseas ministry, health issues, and transition.

One of the exercises we worked through was to reflect on our gains and losses, taking time and space to both grieve and give thanks for all that God had done through our stories. As I reflected on both lists, I was struck by the reality that the gains and the good that come along the way cannot truly be appreciated without acknowledging the hard. God used the hard, the dark, the ugly, as a backdrop to help us to see his goodness and his faithfulness with sharper vision.

A challenge we were given during our retreat was to write out our Hymn of Gratitude to the Lord, and here's mine:

God, you are good, so very good!
Who else is like you?
Who else loves with steadfast love,

Gives mercy, yet is true and holy
and upholds righteousness
In earth and in all heaven?
God, you are a refuge, my refuge!
Who else is like you?
Who else has been there to hide me safe
When the rain poured hard and the thunder crashed
And dreams shattered at my feet?
God, you are faithful, always faithful!
Who else is like you?
Who else keeps his promises
always for generations?
Who can be trusted in the dark
Even when all else seems lost?
You always come through.
You pursue me.
You call me deeper
Because you have called me daughter and friend
And not slave or stranger.
O God, you are Eternal, the Eternal One.
Who else is like you?
Who else does not change
In the midst of the shifting seasons of my days?
To you, oh my God, I give praise!
There is none good like you!
My refuge, the Faithful and Eternal One
Who ever knows and pursues my heart.

# Day 25

*For he knows our frame; he remembers that we are dust.*
*—Psalm 103:14*

"Think of time recently when you disappointed God."

The question, posed to a group of missionaries who had recently returned to the US, didn't sit well with me. Years earlier, a dear friend had challenged my thinking in this area. I owe her much. Her words—more accurately, her quoting God's words—ring in my mind clearly when I'm tempted to believe I'm a disappointment to God.

He knows our frame. He remembers we are dust.

A simple message, yet it changes everything. To be disappointed is to have an expectation that wasn't met in the first place. With this in mind, is there ever anything I can do (or not do) that can truly disappoint my Father?

Does this mean my actions don't have consequences or that he is unconcerned somehow with what I do? Not at all! For example, I can grieve the Holy Spirit by not submitting to his renewing work in my relationships with fellow believers (Ephesians 4:25–32).

Yet still, he remembers. When I mess up (which I will), when I've blown it in a relationship, when I've been selfish, when I've long struggled with pride and he reveals this ugly pattern in my life and I'm overcome with a sense of guilt that threatens to swallow me up and make me want to hide from everyone, it helps to remember that he knows my frame. He remembers. He remembers I am dust. Just dust.

Dust he is transforming and renewing day by day, moment by moment into the image of his Son.

Dust that will deny like Peter and run like Jonah.

Dust that will doubt like Sarah (the one in Genesis and the one writing!) and neglect the good part like Martha.

Yet he will never forget that we are dust. He knows our frame, and he uses us anyway.

He uses us for his glory, and he is not intimidated or thrown off or panicked about what might come of his plan.

He's not even disappointed—because he knew.

By grace through faith in Christ, he chose to call us his own, his workmanship (Ephesians 2:10). He declares us righteous and without condemnation in his sight (Romans 8:1).

And he knew what he was getting into when he chose and redeemed dust.

# Day 26

*Then they cried to the Lord in their trouble,
and he delivered them from their distress.*

*—Psalm 107:6*

Psalm 107 begins with a declaration that God is good, that his steadfast love endures forever. The chapter goes on to give examples of those who have wandered their own way, independent from the Lord. Then out of desperation, they cry out to the Lord, and he faithfully delivers them.

Oh, how I can relate!

In my haste to follow my own way, I often rush ahead of God's leading, believing that I know what's best for me and mine.

Sometimes I ignore God's warning to humble myself.

Sometimes it's a subtle tolerance of "comfortable" sin in some corner of my life (slander, comparison, envy).

Sometimes it's a refusal to forgive or allow God to heal bitterness in my heart.

But *this*. This is what I pray today. Lord, let this be my prayer daily! I cry to you in my trouble, and you, my Lord, are faithful to deliver me from my distress. As verse seven goes on to say: "He led them by a straight way till they reached a city to dwell in." Yes, he is our dwelling place, the one place we find true rest from the crazy and from the wrestling and from the storm.

My hope is in the Lord, and I wait for him alone. In him alone is my soul satisfied, and I will praise him for his steadfast love for me.

# Day 27

*It is in vain that you rise up early and go late to rest, eating the bread of anxious toil; for he gives to his beloved sleep.*
—Psalm 127:2

When our boys were little, I often played a CD a night with a lullaby based on this verse.

I love the simple yet profound truth that it's not up to us to hold the world together while we sleep—that's our Father's job.

It's true in the day too—he gives us rest as a gift from our anxious toil, and we can trust that he will be faithful to work through our weaknesses as we simply obey him one step and one day at a time.

# Day 28

*O Lord, you have searched me and known me!*
—Psalm 139:1

What does it mean to be known by God?

There have been many days in my life when the thought of being known by a Holy God was terrifying to me.

Days when I failed miserably in relationship.

Days when I yelled at my sons for doing something typical for boys their age.

Days when I lost my patience with my husband and blurted out something so disrespectful it seemed to suck the confidence right out of him.

Days when I looked at another mom, on perhaps one of her worst days, and thought "I'd never do that!" then proceeded to rehearse a list of all my accomplishments in motherhood on some of my best.

But to be known, for my heart to be searched by this God so holy, so pure, is a gift.

He takes what is raw and what is rags and what is utterly dark and brings it into the light.

He exposes what lies in the crevices, not so that he may condemn, but so that he may bring light and life to what's broken. His death and life and resurrection brought restoration and redemption for my sins and relationship with God.

Yes, I have decided to give thanks for being known by the light, for he who is light is good and kind.

With my heart open, may God humble me, and may my cry always be "Search me and know me!"

# Day 29

*Let me hear in the morning of your steadfast
love, for in you I trust. Make me know the way
I should go, for to you I lift up my soul.*
—Psalm 143:8

Oh, mornings. My morning routine looks pretty normal on the outside: wake up, roll over, ignore alarm for five minutes; brush teeth and shower; style hair and apply makeup; make coffee and do devotions.

What most people don't know is that this little one-hour block of time is when I fight my toughest battles.

Battles in my mind over past hurts and current realities.

Battles over whether to forgive or hold on to bitterness in my heart.

Battles about my view of myself and God and others around me.

As I look in the mirror every morning, I don't see a brave warrior. I see a war-torn weakling who often stumbles on the battlefield, who drops her weapons when she should take aim, who gets carried away by the bright flags and victory cries of the opposing forces and waves the white flag of surrender much, much too soon.

But, oh, to remember his steadfast love in the morning! To remember that this, *this* is what awaits me when I rise! To know that the battles that rage in real time are deeply connected to these words penned thousands of years ago!

Deep, I soak it in: "Let me hear in the morning of your steadfast love!"

Steadfast when all else is shaky and uncertain.

Steadfast when I am unfaithful and when I stray.

Steadfast even when I don't feel it and always when I don't deserve it.

I arise this morning as a warrior, not because of my own strength or merit but simply because I choose to trust the One who is in control and sovereign over every battle, including this morning.

And every morning, he will show me the way to go.

# Day 30

*Your way was through the sea, your path through the great waters; yet your footprints were unseen.*
—Psalm 77:19

I read once that part of God's being holy is that he is strange, foreign to us in his sovereign wisdom and understanding of the big picture of eternity.

Good? Yes. Loving? The very definition of it. But to say that God's ways are simple or easy to figure out or always comprehensible to us would be foolish and a denial of the awesomeness of the glory of the God we read of in scripture.

So as I find myself in the fog of wondering what he is doing in my own little corner of life, seemingly stuck at times in heartbreaking realities of confusion, grief, pain, and stress of one sort or another, it's there I'm reminded that I serve and am deeply loved and pursued by this great God. This God who always has a plan, who never gets lost, always knows where he's headed and what the plan is.

You see, even when I'm in the fog, he sees the path through the sea.

Through the great waters.

Though the vapor on the surface is enough to make me tremble and fear, he reminds me that the deepest sea will not stand in the way of his plan.

Even when I don't see his footprints, when I can't trace his tracks, he is there.

Take heart, my soul, and be encouraged!

He will never leave your side.

This God is here to stay.

# Day 31

*And he said, "Hagar, servant of Sarai, where have you come from and where are you going?"*

—Genesis 16:8

There's power, at times, in remembering.

There's wisdom to be gained in taking time to reflect on where we've been and where we're headed.

I am often tempted to forget the pain and grief of relationships and parts of me that were left behind when God brought us back to the US, and many days, I wonder if I'll never be the same. Just writing it makes me feel nervous that I will be misunderstood, that my story is insignificant in the scheme of things.

So I move on. I do the work. I stay busy. I forge ahead. I have joy. I do. I enjoy ministry here, and God has been faithful.

But do our stories matter?

God's question to the servant Hagar makes me pause. He knew her story, yet he wanted her to tell it. He first called her by name, then he invited her to recount where she'd been and to articulate where she planned on going. Perhaps he wanted to give her freedom and space to lay it out to understand herself in the scheme of things better than ever before.

It's quite possible that servants—especially female ones—weren't given this luxury of time for critical thinking that we so take for granted today! The angel of the Lord proceeds to give her instruction along with promise in the following verses, affirming that God not only heard her story and her cry but that he valued her as a desperate woman in need of love and care and direction that only he could give.

And what did Hagar learn about herself and about God? "You are a God of seeing." And "Truly here I have seen him who looks after me" (v. 13).

We, like Hagar, can trust that God is inviting us to pour our story at his feet.

Not because he doesn't know it already.

Not because it needs explaining.

Not because we need to justify ourselves before him.

As he invited Hagar, so he invites us: "Where have you come from and where are you going?" Tell him your story and relish in the care he offers. Embrace him as the God who sees you, and rest in your identity as the One who has seen him, the One who ever looks after you and knows the rest of the story.

# About the Author

Sarah Deal was born in Central Florida, where she spent the first two decades of her life in one house. It was here she wrote her first book of poetry, and here, she began to dream of being an author, a missionary, a wife, and a mom.

Over the next two decades, Sarah's dreams were realized when she married her best friend, gave birth to her two sons, and moved across the ocean to serve as a missionary in Indonesia. Here, she and her husband, Shad, thrived in the role of welcoming new teammates to the field, relating to their struggles, and offering a listening ear. Shad served as a housing coordinator and relational liaison, always willing to introduce new people to his local friends. Sarah served as a national language consultant, assisting new teammates to reach fluency in Bahasa Indonesia. Shad and Sarah's own relationships with the local people grew deep, allowing them to build bridges between the two worlds.

But when Shad's epilepsy began to cause frequent, uncontrollable seizures, their family had no choice but to return to the US, leaving nine years of life, dreams, and ministry behind. Two brain surgeries and a long recovery, with no guarantee of seizure freedom, followed. The experiences of grief contrasted with God's grace and goodness promised in his Word have fueled Sarah's desire to write. Her passion has only been kindled to encourage others who have walked a dark road and who, like her, have wrestled with deep questions for their Maker. Her hope is that her writing will inspire others to recognize that they are not alone in their struggle.

Her journey has led her to write *Unfolding*, chronicling the comfort God has so faithfully provided in the midst of difficult seasons. Sarah has spent several years writing monthly articles for Thrive Connection (thriveministry.org/connection) and also posts on her blog weekly at sarahdealwrites.com.

Sarah and Shad, along with their two teenage sons, currently reside in beautiful Lake of the Ozarks, Missouri.

*Thank you for joining me on this journey!*

*To God be the glory,*
*Sarah*

*The unfolding of your words gives light; it imparts understanding to the simple...*
—Psalm 119:130

Visit me at sarahdealwrites.com or email me at indomom4@gmail.com.